THE VEGETABLES WE EAT

BY GAIL GIBBONS

Holiday House / New York

To Michael Cooper,
who eats all his vegetables

.

Special thanks to Becky Grube, Horticultural
Specialist at the University of New Hampshire,
Durham, New Hampshire. Also to Bob Shearer at
Shearer's Greenhouse, Bradford, Vermont.

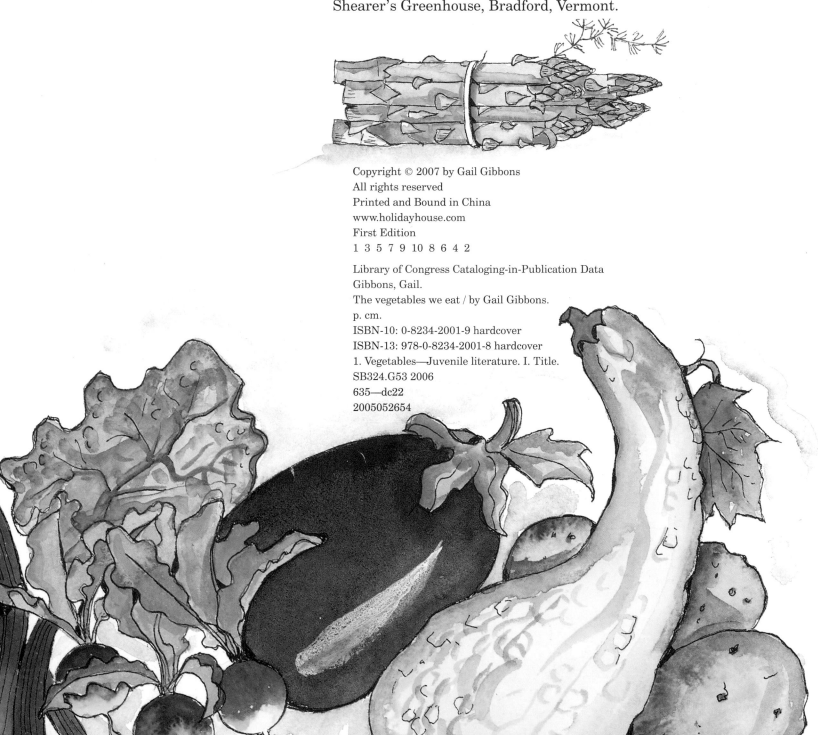

Printed and Bound in China
www.holidayhouse.com
First Edition
1 3 5 7 9 10 8 6 4 2

Library of Congress Cataloging-in-Publication Data
Gibbons, Gail.
The vegetables we eat / by Gail Gibbons.
p. cm.
ISBN-10: 0-8234-2001-9 hardcover
ISBN-13: 978-0-8234-2001-8 hardcover
1. Vegetables—Juvenile literature. I. Title.
SB324.G53 2006
635—dc22
2005052654

PERENNIALS are plants that grow for many growing seasons without having to be replanted.

ANNUALS are plants that grow for only one growing season. They must be replanted to grow again.

Look at all the vegetables! Vegetables are the parts of plants that are grown to be eaten. Most are annuals. Some are perennials.

It is good for us to eat vegetables. They are nutritious and help keep our bodies strong and healthy. They are tasty, too.

We eat vegetables in different ways.

Vegetables grow to be different shapes, sizes, and colors.

LEAF

BULB

FLOWER BUD

ROOT

A BOTANIST is a scientist who studies plants.

TUBER

STEM

FRUIT

SEED

Botanists group the different kinds of vegetables according to the part of the vegetable that is eaten. There are eight groups of vegetables.

LEAF VEGETABLES

ICEBERG LETTUCE

ICEBERG LETTUCE

SOME OTHER LETTUCES . . .

RED LEAF LETTUCE

ROMAINE LETTUCE

BIBB LETTUCE

We eat the leaves of these vegetables.

8

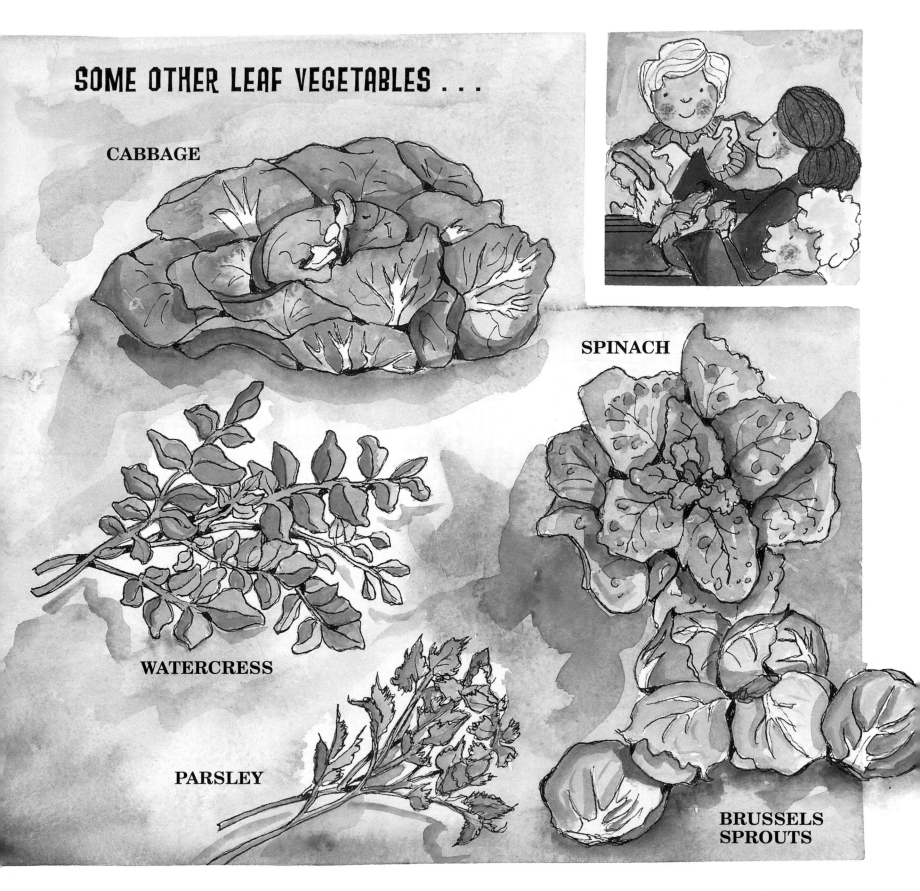

SOME OTHER LEAF VEGETABLES . . .

CABBAGE

SPINACH

WATERCRESS

PARSLEY

BRUSSELS SPROUTS

9

BULB VEGETABLES

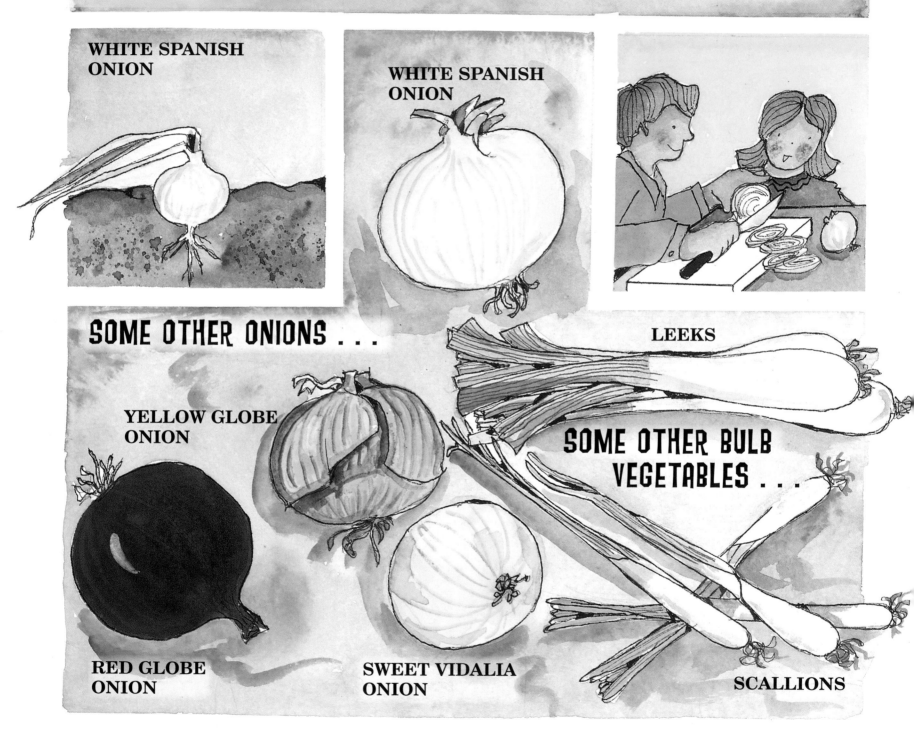

WHITE SPANISH ONION

WHITE SPANISH ONION

SOME OTHER ONIONS . . .

YELLOW GLOBE ONION

LEEKS

SOME OTHER BULB VEGETABLES . . .

RED GLOBE ONION

SWEET VIDALIA ONION

SCALLIONS

We eat the bulbs that grow beneath the ground.

FLOWER BUD VEGETABLES

WHITE SNOWBALL CAULIFLOWER

WHITE SNOWBALL CAULIFLOWER

SOME OTHER CAULIFLOWERS . . .

SOME OTHER FLOWER BUD VEGETABLES . . .

CHEDDAR CAULIFLOWER

PURPLE HEAD CAULIFLOWER

ARTICHOKE

BROCCOLI

The flower buds of these vegetables are eaten.

ROOT VEGETABLES

EARLY WONDER
BEET

EARLY WONDER
BEETS

SOME OTHER BEETS . . .

Some people eat
BEET GREENS.

RED ACE BEETS

DETROIT DARK
RED BEETS

The roots of these vegetables are eaten. They grow beneath
the ground.

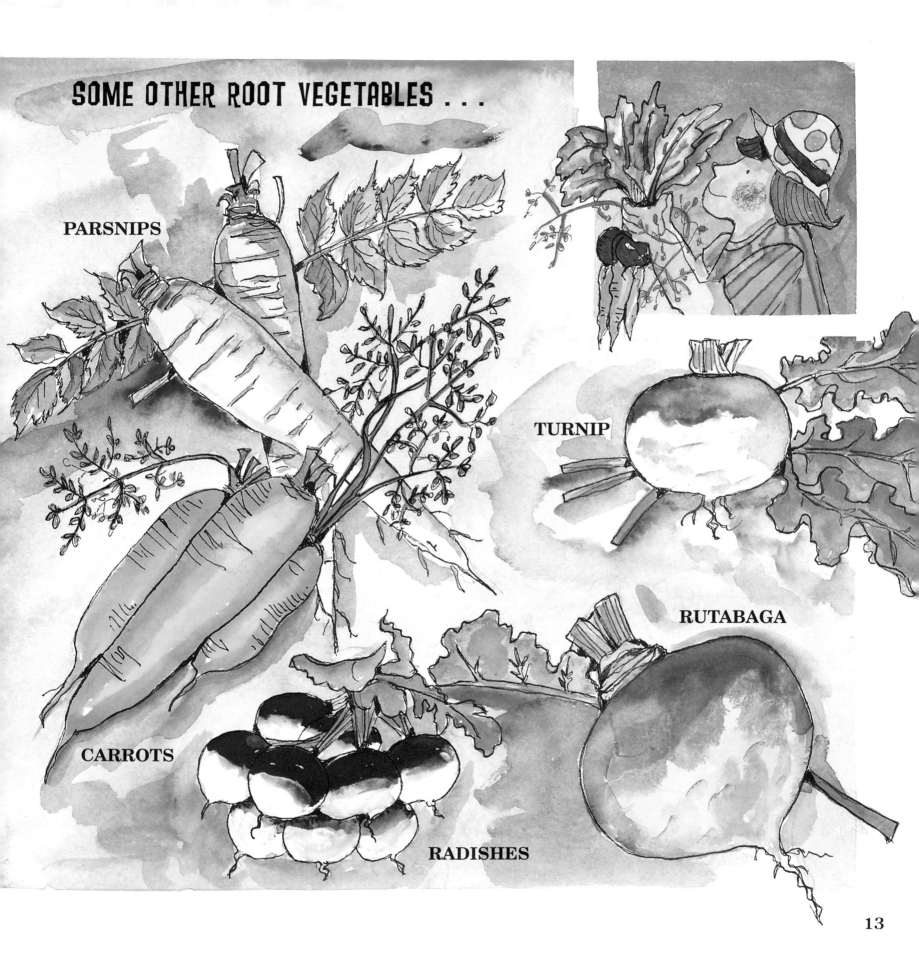

SOME OTHER ROOT VEGETABLES . . .

PARSNIPS

TURNIP

RUTABAGA

CARROTS

RADISHES

TUBER VEGETABLES

KENNEBEC POTATOES

KENNEBEC POTATOES

SOME OTHER POTATOES . . .

RUSSET BURBANK POTATOES

YELLOW YUKON GOLD POTATOES

RED NORLAND POTATOES

PURPLE PERUVIAN POTATOES

The edible part of these vegetables, the tuber, grows beneath the ground.

STEM VEGETABLES

GOLDEN SELF-BLANCHING CELERY

CELERY is an annual.

GOLDEN SELF-BLANCHING CELERY

SOME OTHER CELERIES . . .

FORDHOOK CELERY

GIANT PASCAL CELERY

SOME OTHER STEM VEGETABLES . . .

ASPARAGUS is a perennial.

RHUBARB is a perennial.

The stems of these vegetables are eaten. Some stem vegetables are perennials.

FRUIT VEGETABLES

BEST BOY TOMATOES

BEST BOY TOMATOES

SOME OTHER TOMATOES . . .

BEEFEATER TOMATO

ULTRASWEET TOMATOES

SUGAR PLUM TOMATOES

CHERRY TOMATOES

YELLOW TOMATO

Here are some fruit vegetables that we eat.

SOME OTHER FRUIT VEGETABLES . . .

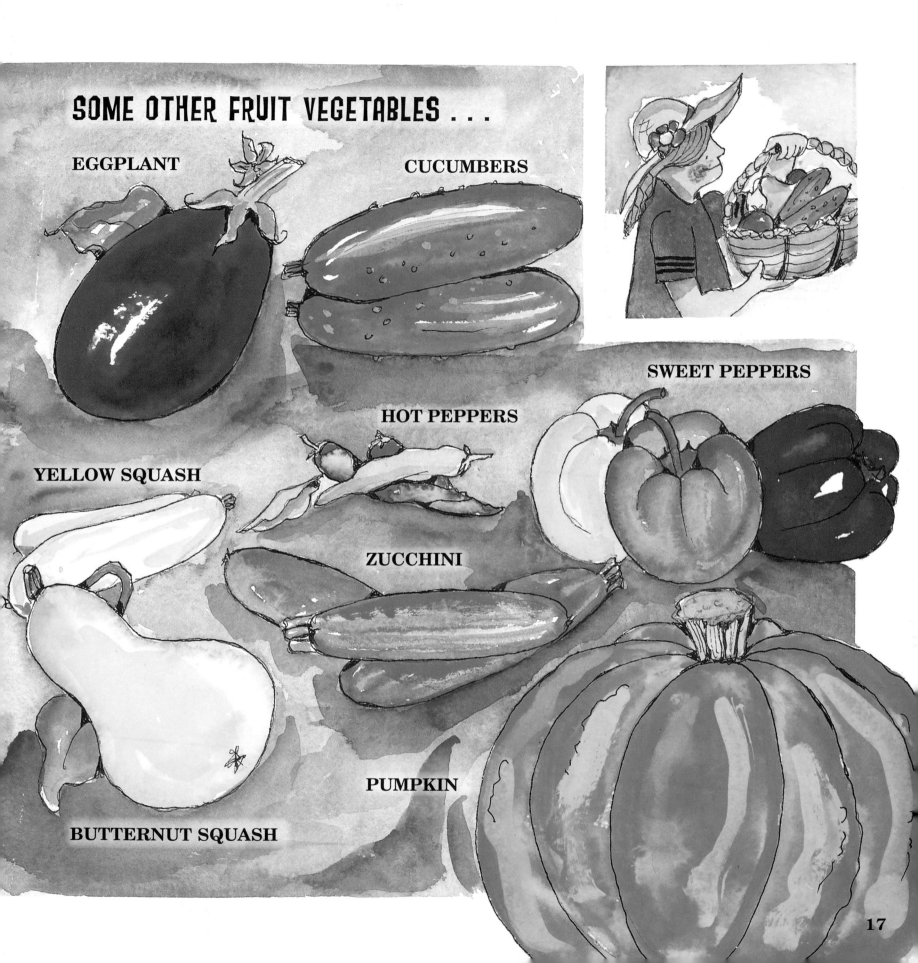

EGGPLANT

CUCUMBERS

SWEET PEPPERS

HOT PEPPERS

YELLOW SQUASH

ZUCCHINI

BUTTERNUT SQUASH

PUMPKIN

17

SEED VEGETABLES

GREEN BEANS

GREEN BEANS

SOME OTHER BEANS . . .

POLE BEANS

LIMA BEANS

YELLOW WAX BEANS

KIDNEY BEANS

NAVY BEANS

We eat the seeds of these plants. Some seed vegetables grow in pods. Sometimes the pods are eaten, too.

18

SOME OTHER SEED VEGETABLES . . .

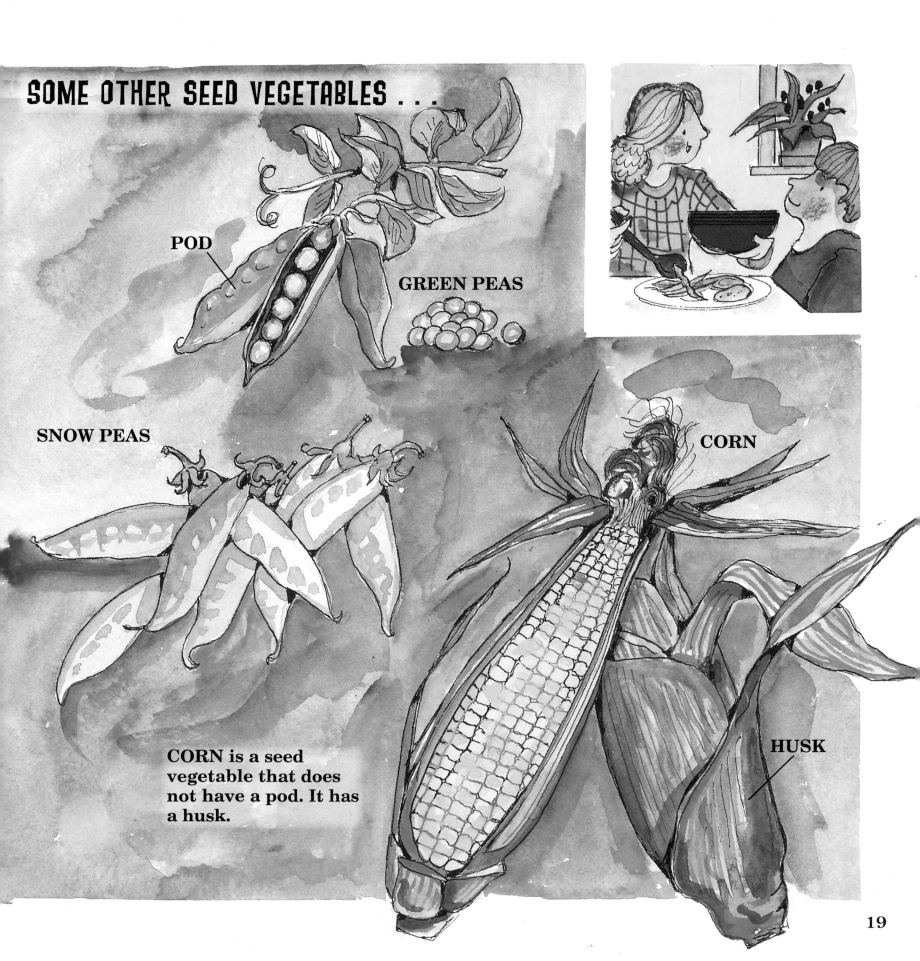

POD

GREEN PEAS

SNOW PEAS

CORN

CORN is a seed vegetable that does not have a pod. It has a husk.

HUSK

19

THE SOYBEAN

SOYBEAN OIL is used to make most household vegetable oils.

LE OIL

SOY MILK

SOY

MARGARINE

SOY SAUCE

SO SA

PAINT

PAINTS

TOFU

TOFU

SOAP

SOAP

CLOTH

PAPER

PLASTICS

Soybeans are a special seed vegetable. They can be used in many ways. Some soybeans are used to make food products. Soybean oil is used to make many nonfood items.

HOW TO GROW YOUR OWN VEGETABLE GARDEN

FERTILIZERS are substances added to the soil as food for plants.

FERTILIZER

A SHOVEL may be used to turn over the soil.

A RAKE may be used to smooth the soil so it is ready for planting.

When it gets warm enough, many people enjoy planting, growing, and later harvesting their own vegetables. Most often they buy packets of seeds that have directions.

Sometimes STRING or STICKS are used to help plant straight rows or to support climbing plants.

When seeds are planted in a circle and covered with a mound of soil, the mound is called a HILL.

STARTER PLANTS

SEEDS

A TROWEL is used to dig small holes for seeds and seedlings.

Some people plant starter plants, also called seedlings. Most of the time vegetable seeds or starter plants are planted in straight rows or in circles.

The garden must be weeded and watered regularly. The plants begin to grow.

In cities, people may grow vegetables in containers.

The vegetable plants will become bigger until they are ready for harvesting.

GREAT BIG VEGETABLE FARMS

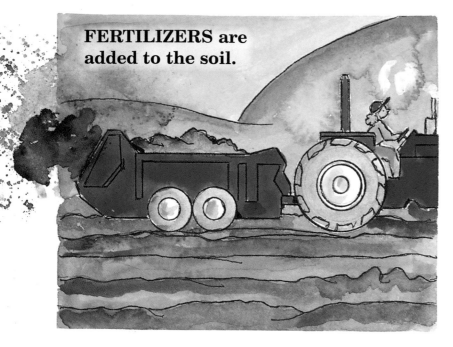

FERTILIZERS are added to the soil.

A PLOW turns over the soil.

A HARROW smoothes the soil so it is ready for planting.

A PLANTER places the seeds in a straight line.

Farmers fertilize the soil. Then the fields are plowed, harrowed, and planted.

26

Some vegetables are picked by hand.

Other vegetables are harvested by machines.

Big sprinkling systems are used to water the vegetable plants. At the end of the growing season, the vegetables are harvested.

Refrigerator trucks haul the vegetables to processing plants. There they will be washed and sorted. Some are frozen, some are canned, and the rest will be sold fresh.

The vegetables are shipped to stores near and far away for people to buy.

At grocery stores fresh vegetables are on display. Canned vegetables line shelves. Frozen vegetables are found in freezers.

Some people buy fresh vegetables at farm stands. It is fun to pick out what to buy. Look at all the delicious vegetables!

VEGETABLES . . . VEGETABLES . . . VEGETABLES . . .

Benjamin Franklin introduced soybean seeds from France to the United States around 1800.

The province of Ontario grows the most vegetables in Canada.

Ontario

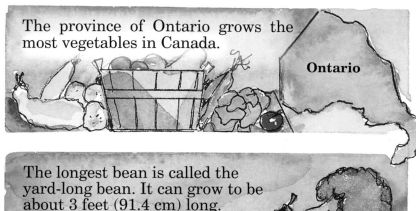

More than half of the world's soybeans are grown in the United States.

The longest bean is called the yard-long bean. It can grow to be about 3 feet (91.4 cm) long.

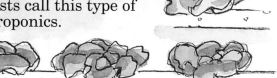

Potato plants originally came from South America.

South America

Vegetables can be grown using water filled with nutrients. No soil is used. Botanists call this type of gardening hydroponics.

There are about 300 different types of potatoes.

300

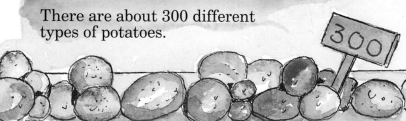

About one-third of all the vegetables grown in the United States come from California.

California

DON'T FORGET . . . it is important to eat vegetables. They are good for you!